HOW TO SOLVE
TIME VALUE OF MONEY PROBLEMS
WITH MS EXCEL® 2016

Alfred L. Kahl, Ph.D., LIFA, CCP

and

William F. Rentz, Ph.D., LIFA

Dedication

To Lola
A.L.K.

To my grandchildren
Abbey, Kaelen, and Andrew
W.F.R.

ABOUT THE AUTHORS

Alfred L. Kahl

Dr. Kahl is a professor of finance (retired) at the Telfer School of Management of the University of Ottawa. He was formerly Associate Dean of Graduate Programs and Director of the MBA Program. He was also a member of the University of Ottawa Pension Plan Committee for 12 years.

Dr. Kahl earned his B.A. from the University of Maryland, his M.B.A. from the University of Pittsburgh, and his Ph.D. from the University of Florida. He is a Licensed International Financial Analyst (LIFA) and is also a Certified Computer Professional (CCP).

William F. Rentz

Dr. Rentz is a professor of finance at the Telfer School of Management of the University of Ottawa. He has served on the University of Ottawa Pension Plan Committee for many years. During his time on the Committee, this pension plan has increased its assets under management from $200 Million to more than $1.5 Billion now and is among the top 100 pension funds in Canada.

Dr. Rentz earned his S.B. from the Massachusetts Institute of Technology (MIT) and his A.M. and Ph.D. from the University of Rochester. He is a Licensed International Financial Analyst (LIFA).

PREFACE

The value of a dollar today is not the same as the value of a dollar tomorrow because if you had a dollar today you could spend it now or invest it to get a return. Thus, the principle of time value of money (TVM) equivalence allows us to compare monetary values from different time periods.

One of the most important uses of time value equivalence is investment decision making. Business managers forecast cash flows from potential investment projects and then discount them to present value to compare that present value with the cost of making the investment. If the net present value is positive, they then make the investment. Individual decision makers use the same procedure when deciding whether to buy a common stock.

This book is a brief and handy guide to the use of Microsoft Excel® 2016 computer spreadsheet software to solve TVM problems that are of the most interest to financial managers and investors.

The Excel spreadsheet software used to prepare this book is part of MS Office 2016, which also includes Word authoring software and PowerPoint presentation software.

Excel 365 Excel Apps, are like Excel 2016 and available not only for the Windows 10 operating system that runs computers, tablets, and telephones, but also for other tablets and smartphones, such as the iPad and iPhone. These Apps are available free to most students with valid educational email addresses.

This book presents step-by-step instructions for solving the most important types of time value of money problems with Excel® along with brief explanations of the relevant financial theory related to the selected problems that are explained herein. Thus, it provides not only the "**how to**" but also the "**why**" of time value of money calculations.

As you work through these examples, you will be building a spreadsheet containing all the examples on the various tabs, so you can then solve any future TVM problems very easily.

TABLE OF CONTENTS

12

CHAPTER 1

ESSENTIAL SPREADSHEET INFORMATION

Introduction

This chapter discusses the basic essential information for spreadsheet use.

The most widely used spreadsheet software is Microsoft Excel®. Your computer was probably delivered with it already installed as part of MS Office®. There are also some free software clones that mimic Excel.

Spreadsheet software replaces columnar paper, pencils, erasers, and calculators in performing repetitive calculations. The software provides a worksheet composed of a flexible matrix of columns and rows which are identified by letters and numbers.

Columns are identified by letters that run horizontally across the top of the worksheet matrix while Rows are identified by numbers that run down the left side of the matrix.

Spreadsheet software is ideal for answering "what if" questions as well as for performing calculations. Once a spreadsheet is set up, input numbers can be changed as desired and the computer will instantly calculate the results. Thus, different alternative courses of action can be investigated.

This chapter discusses the most important spreadsheet information that is needed in the rest of the book.

The Ribbon

Above the worksheet matrix there is a ribbon that serves as a handy way to access the numerous commands that can be used with Excel. This ribbon menu extends across the screen and in most versions of Excel it contains 8 tabs labeled FILE, HOME, INSERT, PAGE LAYOUT, FORMULAS, DATA, REVIEW, and VIEW.

In addition, some third-party software installs even more tabs to the ribbon, but these items are not discussed below.

There is also the Query link labeled ***Tell me what you want to do*** where you can pose a question if you are not sure what to do. If you click on Tell, a popup menu will appear so you can enter your question, and your answer will appear.

HOME

Although HOME is the second tab, it is the default tab location of the ribbon. Here you will find icons for Paste, Cut, Copy, Format Painter, and Clipboard.

Cutting and Pasting can be used to move items while Copy is very useful if you want to copy a formula into other cells. The clipboard can hold items for later copying. The format painter can change the format of cells

Along the Home ribbon you will find icons to change the size and style of the typeface, or the color of cell contents, but most important is the $\sum$AutoSum link at the far right. This can be used to quickly add numbers in a column.

FILE

If you left-click on FILE you will see a menu listing Info, New, Open, Save, Save As, Print, Share, Export, Publish, Close, Account, Options, and Feedback.

Click on Info to protect your worksheet from being changed.

Click on New to start a new blank worksheet.

Click on Open to load a file from your hard drive or the cloud.

Click on Save to save a file to your hard drive or the cloud.

Click on Print to send a spreadsheet to the printer.

Click on Share to send a spreadsheet to someone.

Click on Export to create a PDF or XPS file.

Click on Close to close the current worksheet.

Click on Account to manage your account.

Click on Options to make important changes to how Excel does its work for you. When you click on Options a menu that lists General, Formulas, Proofing, Save, Language, Advanced, Customize Ribbon, Quick Access Toolbar, Add-Ins and Trust Center will appear.

You can then choose Save to tell Excel where to save your files. You probably do not want data files saved on the same default drive as the programs. If you are using a computer, you should have programs on a solid-state C drive and data on a mechanical D drive.

You should also regularly save backups to an external hard drive.

You can choose Add-Ins from the Add-Ins menu. This menu includes 4 headings: Active Application Add-Ins, Inactive Application Add-Ins, Document Related Add-Ins, and Disabled Application Add-Ins.

If the Analysis ToolPak and Solver do not appear under the Active heading they should be listed under the Inactive heading. If these two Add-Ins are not activated, you should activate them immediately because they are extremely useful. To activate any item in this area, click on the GO button, and then check the item you want on the menu that pops up and then click OK.

If you right-click on FILE you will see a menu listing Customize Quick Access Toolbar, Show Quick Access Toolbar below Ribbon, Customize the Ribbon, and Collapse the Ribbon.

You can then left-click on the first one to add icons to the quick access toolbar which is on the top line of the screen. Click on the second to show the quick access icons below the ribbon. Click on the third to add more items to the ribbon. Click on the last item to collapse the ribbon to see more of the screen (not recommended).

INSERT

If you click on INSERT, you will see icons for creating pivot tables and charts. There is also an icon you can click on to access the Windows Store. At the far right, there is a Ω menu for inserting symbols into worksheet cells.

PAGE LAYOUT

If you click on PAGE LAYOUT, you will find links for choosing portrait or landscape mode and for choosing to print the gridlines.

Portrait mode is the default vertical page layout for standard size paper while landscape is the horizontal page layout that is frequently needed for larger spreadsheets, such as those that include 12 months plus totals, for example.

For larger worksheets, it is also possible to specify a particular area of the worksheet to be printed when you do not need the complete printout.

You can also choose to have title headers printed on each page of large worksheets.

FORMULAS

If you click on FORMULAS, you will see that the first icon can be used to insert a formula if you already know which one you want to use.

Click on the next icon to use the AutoSum function.

Click on Recently Used if you want to reuse a formula instead of doing a copy and paste operation.

Click on Financial if you want to choose from among the financial functions.

Click on Logical to use a logical function.

Click on Math & Trig to use one of those functions.

Click on More Functions to access the Statistical or Engineering functions.

DATA

If you click on DATA you will find links for importing external data from the web, cloud, or your other software.

On the right side, there is an Analysis section where you can click on Data Analysis or Solver. Data Analysis is useful for statistical hypothesis testing while Solver can be used iteratively to solve linear programming problems.

REVIEW

If you click on REVIEW, you will find links for the spell checker or translation as well as for choosing to protect parts of the worksheet so no one can make changes.

VIEW

If you click on VIEW, you will find links for zooming or inserting page breaks.

Formula Bar

Just below the ribbon is the function line where the contents of the active cell (the one where the cursor is located) will be displayed. You can inspect the contents of the cell and correct any typo errors in the cell.

Just in front of the line, there is a function icon f_x that can be used to enter a function quickly if you already know which function you need.

Excel 365 App

The Excel App for the iPad and iPhone must be smaller, so it has some of the File icons on the edges of the Ribbon and only Home, Insert, Draw, Formulas, Review and View appear on the Ribbon Tabs. Each of these tabs has fewer options than the computer and laptop versions of Excel 2016, but is otherwise compatible with the examples discussed in this book.

Worksheet Structure

The default Excel 2016 spreadsheet includes only one worksheet which is identified as Sheet 1 on the tab at the bottom left edge of the worksheet.

Additional worksheet tabs can be added as needed by clicking on the plus sign located just to the right of the tab.

You can insert names into these tabs. For example, it is possible to use 12 monthly tabular worksheets and accumulate the monthly totals from those worksheets into the main yearly worksheet. Just right click on the tab and then choose Rename on the pop-up menu. Other choices on the menu include: Insert, Delete, Move or Copy, View Code, Protect Sheet, Tab Color, Hide, and Select All Sheet.

The worksheet format includes a matrix of cells. The matrix includes a horizontal listing of the column letters along the top of the matrix just below the Ribbon as well as a vertical listing of the row numbers down the left side of the worksheet.

Each cell is identified by its location at the intersection of a column and a row, for example, cell A3 is located at the intersection of column A and row 3.

Cells may contain labels (of text) or values (numbers) or formulas, which are instructions to perform calculations.

Thus, a portion of a sample worksheet would look like this:

	A	B	C
1			
2			
3			
4			
5			
6			

It is recommended to separate the input data from the intermediate calculations and the results. Thus, the input variables should be entered in a top or left side data area so they can be easily changed.

Formulas for the intermediate calculations and the results normally should be entered in separate areas using formulae that use the locations of the input data cells rather than numbers contained in the cells.

For example, the formula =*A2+A3* in cell A4 indicates that the computer should add the numbers located in cells A2 and A3 and display the result in cell A4.

	A	B	C
1	Data		
2	2		
3	3		
4	5		
5			
6			

If you click on cell A4, you will see the formula =*A2+A3* displayed in the formula bar above the matrix.

Alternatively, you can get the same formula in cell A4 by clicking on the *fx* symbol just in front of the formula bar.

CHAPTER 2

TVM CALCULATIONS: LUMP SUMS

Introduction

The essence of time value of money (TVM) calculations is to determine a **time value equivalence** given a rate of interest or discount.

The most basic principle of the time value of money (TVM) is that a dollar today is worth more than a dollar in one year or at any future time. If one has a dollar today, one can invest that dollar to earn more than a dollar to be received in one year.

For example, if one could earn 10% in one year, then a dollar today is time value equivalent to $1 x 1.10 = $1.10 one year from now.

If 10% is also the prevailing interest rate in the second year and interest is compounded annually, then $1 today is also time value equivalent to $1.00 x $1.10^2 = $1.21 in two years.

The dollar today is referred to as a present value (PV). The $1.10 would be the time value equivalent future value (FV) in one year. The $1.21 would be the time value equivalent FV in two years.

Time Value of Money (TVM) Variables

The TVM variables for basic financial calculations are:

Rate of interest or discount rate (RATE),
Number of periods (NPER),
Periodic payments (PMT),
Present value (PV), and
Future value (FV).

In general, TVM problems involve these five variables.

Usually four are known and the fifth is unknown but some problems can be solved with only 3 variables.

This chapter discusses TVM calculations using only lump sums, so there are no periodic payments (PMT).

The next chapter will introduce even periodic cash flows into TVM calculations.

To simplify the discussions, taxes are ignored in all the examples used throughout this book.

Example 1: FV (Lump Sum Loan Repayment)

What is the future value (FV) of $7,091.90 at the end of 4 years, if the interest rate is compounded annually at 5%? That is, if you borrowed $7,091.90 today at an annual compound interest rate of 5%, how much money would you have to repay in four years?

How to Construct a Spreadsheet Worksheet

To construct a simple worksheet for time value of money calculations, begin by putting the labels INPUTS, TVM, and SOLUTION in the three column headings of row 1 in cells A1, B1, and C1, respectively.

Then in column B starting with cell B2, enter the labels for the five TVM variables (RATE, NPER, PMT, PV and FV). Note that in Excel language, the number of periods is indicated by NPER.

To remind us that this column remains constant, format it to be bolded by highlighting the column from cell B1 to B6

and then clicking on the B for bold icon on the ribbon.
Then click on the centering icon on the ribbon to format the
column items to be centered.

The worksheet should now look like this:

	A	B	C
1	INPUTS	**TVM**	SOLUTION
2		**RATE**	
3		**NPER**	
4		**PMT**	
5		**PV**	
6		**FV**	

Enter 5% in cell A2.

Enter 4 in cell A3.

Enter 7091.90 in cell A5.

Enter the formula *=A5*(1+A2)^A3* in cell C6. Build this
formula by clicking on the cells where the data has been
entered. This will minimize typing and make the formula
more versatile because you can later change the inputs to
solve new problems.

The * symbol in Excel language means to multiply.

The ^ symbol in Excel language means to raise the number within the parentheses to the exponential value located in the cell A3.

Then the future value, FV, will appear as $1,061.21 if the cell C6 is formatted for currency format with two decimal places. To format the cell, right click on cell C6 and then left click on Format Cells. On the Number Tab, left click on Currency. Then left click on the OK button on the lower right side of the menu.

The worksheet will now look like this if you expand the width of column C by placing your cursor on the right edge and moving it to the right:

	A	B	C
1	INPUTS	TVM	SOLUTION
2	5%	RATE	
3	4	NPER	
4		PMT	
5	7091.90	PV	
6		FV	-$8,620.25

Thus, the PV = $7,091.90 borrowed today is time value equivalent to $8,620.25 to be paid back in 4 years when the interest rate is 5% compounded annually.

Excel Functions

Formulas can be inserted into the worksheet more easily by using the built-in Excel functions to create the formulas. Move the cursor to cell C6 and click on it.

Then look upward to find the Formulas tab on the Ribbon Menu. Click on Formulas, then click on Financial and then click on FV.

Click on the Rate box, and then click on cell A2.
Click on the Nper box, and then click on cell A3.
Click on the Pmt box, and then click on cell A4.
Click on the Pv box, and then click on cell A5.
Click OK.

The formula =*FV(A2,A3,A4,A5)* will now be entered into the cell C6 and the value -$8,620.25 will be displayed there.

Note that cell A4 in this example is empty. In general, however, there can be a value other than 0 for the PMT in cell A4. Thus, we prefer to include cell A4 in the function because we want the model to work generally. Otherwise, you should enter zero in the cell.

Excel Function Wizard

There is another way to find Excel® functions. You can use the Function Wizard. Move the cursor to cell C6 and click on it. Then look upward to find $\sum$ AutoSum $\downarrow$ on the right side of the menu. Click on the arrow and it will show several of the functions most recently used. If the function you want is shown, you can choose it. Otherwise click on the bottom entry More Functions, then type the name of the function you want or a description of what you want to do in the search box, and click on GO. The wizard will then find the function for you and you can fill in the boxes as described in the preceding section:

Click on the Rate box, and then click on cell A2.
Click on the Nper box, and then click on cell A3.
Click on the Pmt box, and then click on cell A4.

Click on the Pv box, and then click on cell A5.

Click OK.

The formula $=FV(A2,A3,A4,A5)$ will then be entered into the cell C6 by the function wizard, and the value $1,061.21 will be displayed. This is the same result obtained by the Formula method described in the preceding section.

Enter a name for this worksheet on the Tab, such as X1FV, and save it.

Example 2: PV (What Can You Borrow Now?)

How much can you borrow today if a lump sum repayment of $8,620.25 is due in 4 years and the interest rate is 5% compounded annually?

Copy the Example 1 worksheet and paste it to another tab. The worksheet now looks like this:

	A	B	C
1	INPUTS	TVM	SOLUTION
2	5%	RATE	
3	4	NPER	
4		PMT	
5	7091.90	PV	
6		FV	-$8,620.25

Enter 5% in cell A2.

Enter 4 in cell A3.

Delete the contents of cell A5.

Enter -8620.25 in cell A6.

Move the cursor to cell C5 and click on it. Then look upward to find the Formulas tab on the Ribbon Menu. Click on Formulas; then click on Financial, and then click on PV.

Click on the Rate box, and then click on cell A2.
Click on the Nper box, and then click on cell A3.
Click on the Pmt box, and then click on cell A4.
Click on the Fv box, and then click on cell A6.
Click OK.

The formula *=PV(A2,A3,A4,A6)* will now be entered into the cell C5 and the value $7,091.90 will be displayed there.

Delete the contents of cell C6.

The worksheet now looks like this:

	A	B	C
1	INPUTS	TVM	SOLUTION
2	5%	RATE	
3	4	NPER	
4		PMT	
5		PV	$7,091.90
6	-8620.25	FV	

In other words, a PV today of $7,091.90 is time value equivalent to $8,620.25 in 4 years at an annual compound interest rate of 5%. This time value equivalence, of course, is consistent with the result of Example 1.

The process of finding a present value is referred to as **discounting**. In this case the relevant periodic interest rate is often called the **discount rate**.

Enter a name for this worksheet on the Tab, such as X2PV, and save it.

Example 3: Rate of Return or Growth Rate

Assume an asset can be purchased today for $7,091.90. It will return a lump sum payment of $8,620.25 at the end of 4 years. What rate of return would you earn if you bought this asset?

Copy the Example 2 worksheet and paste it to another tab. The worksheet looks like this:

	A	B	C
1	INPUTS	TVM	SOLUTION
2	5%	RATE	
3	4	NPER	
4		PMT	
5		PV	$7,091.90
6	-8620.25	FV	

Delete the contents of cell A2.

Enter -7091.90 in cell A5.

Enter 8620.25 in cell A6.

Delete the contents of cell C5.

Now we need to create a formula in cell C2 to tell Excel to calculate the RATE. Move the cursor to cell C2 and click on it. Then look upward to find the Formulas tab on the Ribbon Menu. Click on Formulas, then click on FV and the drop-down menu will appear.

Click on the Nper box, and then click on cell A3.
Click on the Pmt box, and then click on cell A4.
Click on the Pv box, and then click on cell A5.
Click on the Fv box, and then click on cell A6.
Click OK.

The formula *=RATE(A3,A4,A5,A6)* will now be entered into the cell C2 and the value 5% will be displayed there.

The worksheet will now look like this if the cell C2 is formatted to percentage and right justified. To format the cell, right click on cell C2 and then left click on Format Cells. On the Percentage Tab, choose 2 decimal places. Then left click on the OK button on the lower right side of the menu. To justify cells, highlight them and click on the right justification icon on the Home ribbon.

	A	B	C
1	INPUTS	TVM	SOLUTION
2		RATE	5.00%
3	4	NPER	
4		PMT	
5	-7091.90	PV	
6	8620.25	FV	

This rate of return calculation is consistent with the time value equivalents determined in Examples 1 and 2 and is called an **internal rate of return** (IRR).

So long as the cash flows of a problem conform to the structure of the RATE function (i.e. a PV, level periodic payments, and an FV with a least two of these variables being non-zero with opposite signs), the RATE function can be used to calculate the IRR.

Later in this book, we will use the IRR function in a more complex problem where periodic payments are **not** level.

In this example, -7,091.90 represents the money invested (i.e. an outflow) to buy the asset, and the 8,620.25 represents the money returned (i.e. an inflow) when the asset matures.

Entering the PV and FV with opposite signs is consistent with the sign convention discussed in Examples 1 and 2 above. If you enter both values as **positive** numbers, you will receive the **#NUM!** error message!

Note that this rate of return can also be viewed as the **growth rate** of your asset value due to compounding. **Often investors wish to know the growth rate of the dividends of a share of stock over time.**

The RATE function can be used to find this compound dividend growth rate which is used to value a share of common stock.

Enter a name for this worksheet on the Tab, such as X3RATE, and save it.

Now suppose you learn that the asset will actually cost $7,146.19 instead of $7,091.90. What rate of return will you earn?

You could just enter -7146.19 in cell A5 to change the PV. Then Excel will recalculate the worksheet and the rate 4.80% will be displayed in cell C2 if it is formatted for percentage with 2 decimal places.

To format the cell, right click on cell C2 and then left click on Format Cells. Left click on the Percentage Tab (2 decimal places are the default). Then left click on the OK button on the lower right side of the menu.

The worksheet will now look like this:

	A	B	C
1	INPUTS	TVM	SOLUTION
2		RATE	4.80%
3	4	NPER	
4		PMT	
5	-7146.19	PV	
6	8620.25	FV	

If you pay **more** for the asset, you earn a **lower** rate of return on it. The important thing, though, is that you can do "what if" analyses with Excel.

However, if instead of losing the first result using $7,091.90, you want to be able to compare both worksheets side-by-side, you could instead just copy the whole matrix from cells A1 to C6 and paste it into another area of the spreadsheet starting from, say cells E1 to G6. Then you could enter -7146.19 in cell E5 to change the PV and Excel will recalculate the worksheet and the rate 4.80% will be displayed in cell G2.

Then save this worksheet again, so you can use it again for similar problems.

Example 4: NPER to Reach a Goal (Home)

Suppose you have inherited $30,000 from your late Uncle Jack, but you will need $36,500 to make a down payment on your dream home. If you can invest this lump sum of $30,000 at 4% compounded annually, how long will it take to reach your financial goal?

Copy the Example 3 spreadsheet and paste it to another tab. The worksheet looks like this:

	A	B	C
1	INPUTS	**TVM**	SOLUTION
2		**RATE**	5.00%
3	4	**NPER**	
4		**PMT**	
5	-7091.90	**PV**	
6	8620.25	**FV**	

Enter 4% in cell A2.

Delete the contents of cell A3.

Enter -30000 in cell A5.

Enter 36500 in cell A6.

Delete the contents of cell C2.

We now need to insert a formula in cell C3 to tell the computer to calculate the NPER. Move the cursor to cell C3 and left click on it. Then look upward to find the Formulas tab on the Ribbon Menu. Click on Formulas. Then click on Financial. Then click on FV. The drop-down menu will appear.

Click on the Rate box, and then click on cell A2.
Click on the Pmt box, and then click on cell A4.
Click on the Pv box, and then click on cell A5.
Click on the Fv box, and then click on cell A6.
Click OK.

The formula *=NPER(A2,A4,A5,A6)* will now be entered into the cell C3 and the value 5.00% will be displayed there if the cell is formatted for 2 decimal places.

You can format the cell by clicking on it, and choosing number as the format style and selecting 2 as the number of decimal places.

The worksheet will now look like this:

	A	B	C
1	INPUTS	**TVM**	SOLUTION
2	4%	**RATE**	
3		**NPER**	5.00
4		**PMT**	
5	-30000	**PV**	
6	36500	**FV**	

Thus, 5 is the number of periods required to achieve your financial goal.

Enter a name for this worksheet on the Tab, such as X4NPER, and save it.

Example 5: NPER to Reach a Goal (Retire)

Let us consider another example of savings for a financial goal. Suppose you feel that you will need at least $1,000,000 in savings to adequately fund your retirement. You currently have $30,000 in savings, and you are 21 years old. If you can invest this lump sum at 8% compounded annually, at what age can you afford to retire?

Copy the Example 4 worksheet and paste it to a new tab. The worksheet looks like this:

	A	B	C
1	INPUTS	TVM	SOLUTION
2	4%	RATE	
3		NPER	5.00
4		PMT	
5	-30000	PV	
6	36500	FV	

Enter 8% in cell A2.

Enter 1000000 in cell A6.

Excel will recalculate the worksheet immediately and it will now look like this:

	A	B	C
1	INPUTS	TVM	SOLUTION
2	8%	RATE	
3		NPER	45.56
4		PMT	
5	-30000	PV	
6	1000000	FV	

Thus, NPER now equals 45.56. So, if you can set aside $30,000 at age 21, you can retire at age 21 + 45.56, which is approximately age 67!

Enter a name for this worksheet on the Tab, such as X5NPER, and save it.

In the current very low interest rate environment, an 8% return is **not** achievable by investing in relatively low risk securities such as government bonds.

A more reasonable rate to assume is 4%. Replacing 8 with 4 in cell A2 will cause Excel to recalculate and now the worksheet will look like this:

	A	B	C
1	INPUTS	**TVM**	SOLUTION
2	4%	**RATE**	
3		**NPER**	89.41
4		**PMT**	
5	-30000	**PV**	
6	1000000	**FV**	

Thus, now NPER equals 89.41 years, so you can retire at approximately age $21 + 89 = 110$.

Given current life expectancies, it appears that your financial plan is **not** feasible in your lifetime!

This suggests that you must plan to make periodic deposits to your savings account throughout your working career rather than a single lump sum deposit today.

CHAPTER 3

TVM CALCULATIONS:

EVEN CASH FLOWS

Introduction

This chapter discusses the time value of money (TVM) calculations with even cash flows of ordinary annuities and annuities due.

An **ordinary** or **regular annuity** is a series of even cash flows at the **end** of each period for a specified number of periods. Auto loans and home mortgages are the major loans by dollar amount for most consumers and are examples of ordinary annuities.

An **annuity due** is a series of level periodic payments at the **beginning** of each period for a specified number of periods. Lease payments for automobiles and apartments as well insurance premiums are examples of annuities due.

Timelines are often used to visualize TVM problems. Example 6 below illustrates the use of a timeline.

Example 6: FV of an Ordinary Annuity (Savings)

Suppose that you wish to deposit $2,000 at the end of each year for 4 years. What is the FV of this annuity if the interest rate is 5 percent compounded annually? That is, how much money have you accumulated in your savings account at the end of 4 years?

The timeline below represents an ordinary annuity for 4 years of $2,000 per year using an annual interest rate of 5%.

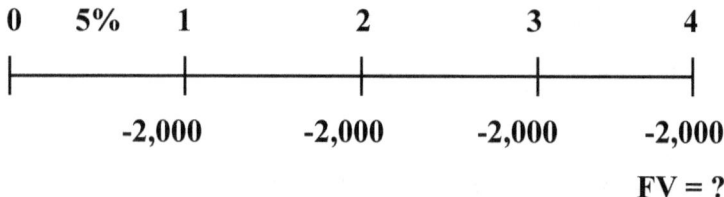

The four deposits of $2,000 must be entered into the worksheet as negative numbers because these cash flows are considered to be outflows. Each deposit will earn 5% annual interest until the end of the four-year period.

Copy the Example 1 FV spreadsheet and paste it to another tab. The worksheet now looks like this:

	A	B	C
1	INPUTS	TVM	SOLUTION
2	5%	RATE	
3	4	NPER	
4		PMT	
5	7091.90	PV	
6		FV	-$8,620.25

Enter -2000 in cell A4.

Delete the contents of cell A5.

The worksheet now looks like this:

	A	B	C
1	INPUTS	TVM	SOLUTION
2	5%	RATE	
3	4	NPER	
4	-2000	PMT	
5		PV	
6		FV	$8,620.25

The ordinary annuity of $2,000 per year for 4 years is time value equivalent at a 5% annual interest rate to a lump sum FV of $8,620.25 at the end of 4 years. Note that this is the FV computed in Example 1. This means that this ordinary annuity is also time value equivalent to the PV of $7,091.90 originally borrowed in Example 1.

Enter a name for this worksheet on the Tab, such as X6FVA, and save it.

Example 7: FV of an Annuity Due (Savings)

Redo Example 6 above as an annuity due. Recall that each payment of an annuity due occurs at the beginning of the period instead of at the end as with an ordinary or regular annuity. In essence, each payment occurs one period sooner.

The timeline below represents an annuity due of $2,000 per year for 4 years using an annual interest rate of 5%.

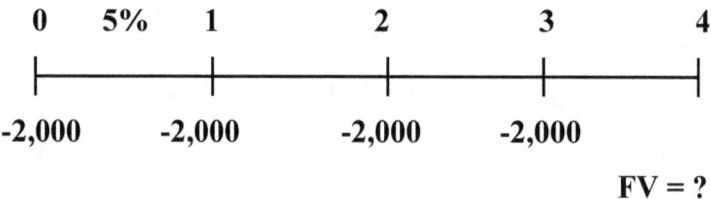

Copy the worksheet from Example 6 and paste it to another tab. The worksheet now looks like this:

	A	B	C
1	INPUTS	TVM	SOLUTION
2	5%	RATE	
3	4	NPER	
4	-2000	PMT	
5		PV	
6		FV	$8,620.25

Modify the formula in cell C6 which now reads =FV(A2,A3,A4,A5) to read =FV(A2,A3,A4,A5)*(1+A2) by editing the formula line which appears just after the *fx* symbol. The value 9,051.26 will be displayed immediately by the computer and the worksheet will now look like this:

	A	B	C
1	INPUTS	TVM	SOLUTION
2	5%	RATE	
3	4	NPER	
4	-2000	PMT	
5		PV	
6		FV	$9,051.26

Note that the FV= 9,051.26 of the annuity due is larger than the FV = 8,620.25 for the ordinary annuity.

This is because **each** payment of the annuity due is earning interest for 1 additional period.

Thus, the FV of the annuity due equals the FV of the ordinary annuity **times** (1 + periodic interest rate), *viz.*, $9,051.26 = $8,620.25 x (1 + 0.05).

Note also that the formula line can be modified more simply by changing the *=FV(A2,A3,A4,A5)* formula to read *=FV(A2,A3,A4,A5,1)* because this will change the function to the annuity due mode.

Enter a name for this worksheet on the Tab, such as X7FVAD, and save it.

Example 8: PV of an Annuity (Borrowing)

What is the PV of the ordinary annuity in Example 6 above? That is, how much can you borrow today if you can repay $2,000 at the end of each year for 4 years when the compound annual interest rate is 5%?

The timeline below represents an ordinary annuity of $2,000 per year for 4 years using an annual interest rate of 5%.

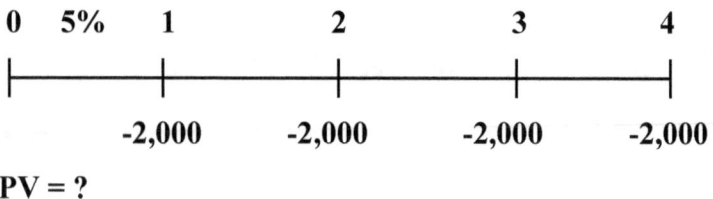

PV = ?

Copy the Example 2 worksheet and paste it to a new tab.

The worksheet now looks like this:

	A	B	C
1	INPUTS	TVM	SOLUTION
2	5%	RATE	
3	4	NPER	
4		PMT	
5		PV	$7,091.90
6	-8620.25	FV	

Enter -2000 in cell A5 and delete the entry in cell A6.

Now the worksheet looks like this:

	A	B	C
1	INPUTS	TVM	SOLUTION
2	5%	RATE	
3	4	NPER	
4	-2000	PMT	
5		PV	$7,091.90
6		FV	

Note that the PV of 7,091.90 of this ordinary annuity is smaller than the FV of the ordinary annuity of 8,620.25 calculated in Example 6. **This is always true for any annuity evaluated with a positive interest rate.**

In this example, when interest is compounded at 5% annually, we have shown that the ordinary annual annuity of $2,000 for 4 years is time value equivalent to a PV of 7,091.90.

In Example 6, we showed that this same annuity is time value equivalent to an FV = 8,620.25 at the end of year 4. Thus, a PV = 7,091.90 must be time value equivalent to an FV = 8,620.25 at the end of year 4 when interest is compounded annually at 5%. Recall that we had already shown this time value equivalence in Examples 1 and 2 of Chapter 1.

Enter a name for this worksheet on the Tab, such as X8PVA, and save it.

Example 9: PV of an Annuity Due (Leasing)

Redo Example 8 as an annuity due.

The timeline below represents an annuity due of $2,000 per year for 4 years using an annual interest rate of 5%.

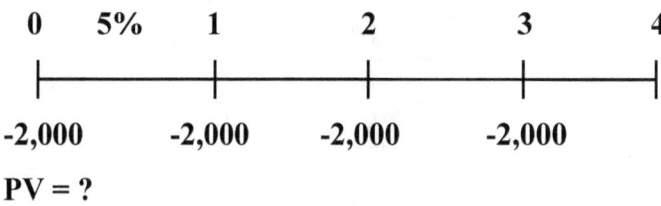

0	5%	1	2	3	4

-2,000   -2,000   -2,000   -2,000

PV = ?

Copy and paste the Example 8 worksheet to a new tab. The worksheet now looks like this:

	A	B	C
1	INPUTS	TVM	SOLUTION
2	5%	RATE	
3	4	NPER	
4	-2000	PMT	
5		PV	$7,091.90
6		FV	

Modify the formula =*PV(A2,A3,A4,A5* in cell C5 to read
=*PV(A2,A3,A4,A5)*(1+A2)* by editing the formula line
which appears just after the *fx* symbol and the worksheet
will now look like this:

	A	B	C
1	INPUTS	TVM	SOLUTION
2	5%	RATE	
3	4	NPER	
4	-2000	PMT	
5		PV	$7,446.50
6		FV	

Note also that the formula line can be modified more
simply by changing the =*PV(A2,A3,A4,A6)* formula to read
=*PV(A2,A3,A4,A6,1)* since this will change the function to
the annuity due mode.

Instead of the previous result of 7,091.50 in Example 8, we
now have 7,446.50. Note that 7,091.90 x 1.05 = 7,446.50,
where 7,091.90 is the PV of the ordinary annuity found in
Example 8.

Whether you are calculating the PV or the FV of an annuity due, the annuity due value is always (1 + the periodic interest rate) times the corresponding value for the ordinary annuity.

In other words, when computing the FV of an annuity due in comparison to an ordinary annuity, **every annuity due payment earns interest for 1 more period.**

Similarly, when computing the PV of an annuity due in comparison to an ordinary annuity, **every annuity due payment gets discounted for 1 less period.** The effect is the same.

For any positive interest rate, the value of the ordinary annuity understates the value of the corresponding annuity due by the factor (1 + periodic interest rate).

Enter a name for this worksheet on the Tab, such as X9PVAD, and save it.

Example 10: Rate of Return (Ordinary Annuity)

Suppose that you are offered the opportunity to invest $3,000 at the end of each year for the next 3 years. You are promised a return of $10,000 at the end of three years. You require a rate of return of 10% for investment of this degree of risk. Should you make this investment?

The timeline below represents an ordinary annuity for 3 years of $3,000 per year using an annual interest rate of ?%.

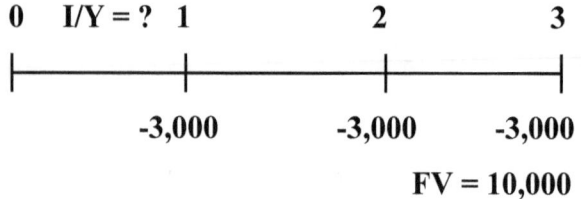

Copy the Example 3 worksheet and paste it to a new tab.

The worksheet now looks like this:

	A	B	C
1	INPUTS	TVM	SOLUTION
2		RATE	5.00%
3	4	NPER	
4		PMT	
5	-7091.90	PV	
6	8620.25	FV	

Enter 3 in cell A3.

Enter -3000 in cell A4.

Enter 10000 in cell A6.

Now the worksheet looks like this:

	A	B	C
1	INPUTS	TVM	SOLUTION
2		RATE	10.73%
3	3	NPER	
4	-3000	PMT	
5		PV	
6	10000	FV	

Thus, the investment earns an internal rate of return (IRR) of 10.73%, which is greater than your required rate of return of 10%. Hence, you should make the investment.

Enter a name for this worksheet on the Tab, such as X10RATEA, and save it.

Example 11: Rate of Return (Annuity Due)

Recalculate the rate of return for Example 10 when the payments are at the beginning of the period. Recall that you now are offered the opportunity to invest $3,000 at the beginning of each year for the next 3 years. You require a rate of return of 10% for investment of this degree of risk. Should you make this investment now if your required rate of return is still 10%?

The timeline below represents an annuity due of $3,000 per year for 3 years using an annual interest rate of ?%.

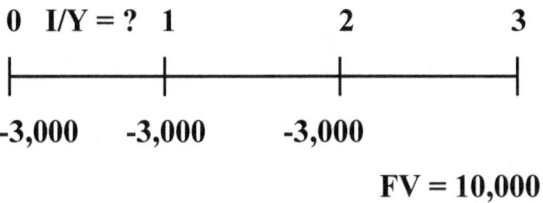

0   I/Y = ?   1   2   3

-3,000   -3,000   -3,000

FV = 10,000

Copy the Example 10 worksheet and paste it to a new tab. The worksheet now looks like this:

	A	B	C
1	INPUTS	TVM	SOLUTION
2		RATE	10.73%
3	3	NPER	
4	-3000	PMT	
5		PV	
6	10000	FV	

Modify the formula *=RATE(A3,A4,A5,A6)* in cell C2 to read *=RATE(A3,A4,A5,A6,1)* by editing the formula line which appears just after the *fx* symbol. This changes the calculation to annuity due mode.

The worksheet will now look this this:

	A	B	C
1	INPUTS	TVM	SOLUTION
2		RATE	5.36%
3	3	NPER	
4	-3000	PMT	
5		PV	
6	10000	FV	

Thus, the rate of return is 5.36%.

Since your required rate of return is still 10%, you should **not** make this investment because your IRR is less than your required rate of return. The IRR is lower because you must make each of the periodic payments 1 period earlier, and this makes the investment unattractive in this example.

Enter a name for this worksheet on the Tab, such as X11RATEAD, and save it.

Example 12: Yield to Maturity (YTM) of a Bond

Consider a bond that matures in 20 years (i.e. 40 semi-annual periods), has a stated coupon rate of 10%, and is now selling for $900. What is the yield to maturity (YTM) for this bond?

Bonds typically have maturity values of $1,000. (Sometimes the maturity value is referred to as the face value or par value of the bond.) Most bonds have a stated nominal annual coupon rate, but the interest payments are usually made semi-annually at ½ of the stated rate. Thus, these payments are a semi-annual ordinary annuity during the life of the bond. For the typical bond, the YTM is a nominal annual interest rate based on semi-annual compounding just like the stated coupon interest rate. The YTM calculation is a type of IRR calculation. The timeline is:

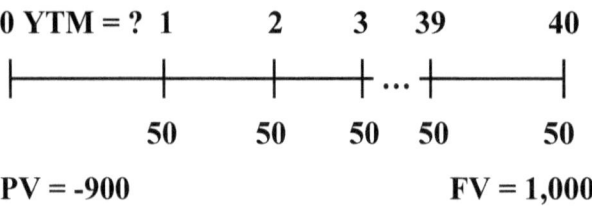

Copy the Example 10 worksheet and paste it to a new tab. The worksheet now looks like this:

	A	B	C
1	INPUTS	TVM	SOLUTION
2		RATE	10.73%
3	3	NPER	
4		PMT	
5	-3000	PV	
6	10000	FV	

Enter 40 in cell A3.

Enter 50 in cell A4.

Enter -900 in cell A5.

Enter 1000 in cell A6.

Modify the formula =*RATE(A3,A4,A5,A6)* in cell C2 to read =*RATE(A3,A4,A5,A6)*2* by editing the formula line which appears just after the *fx* symbol. This multiplication is necessary because the payments are semi-annual (twice a year).

Now the worksheet looks like this:

	A	B	C
1	INPUTS	TVM	SOLUTION
2		RATE	11.27%
3	40	NPER	
4	50	PMT	
5	-900	PV	
6	1000	FV	

Thus, the YTM for this bond is 11.27%. This should be compared to your required rate of return to determine if this is an attractive investment. So, if you require an YTM of 11% for investments of this degree of risk, then this bond is an attractive investment because it exceeds your required rate of return. Note that the YTM was **more** than the stated coupon interest rate.

Whenever the selling price of the bond is less than the maturity value, the YTM will be more than the coupon interest rate and vice versa.

Enter a name for this worksheet on the Tab, such as X12YTM, and save it.

Example 13: Price (PV) of a Bond

This example demonstrates that if the YTM is **less** than the coupon rate, the bond will sell for **more** than its maturity value.

Consider a bond that matures in 20 years and has a stated coupon rate of 10%. For a bond of this degree of riskiness, you require a yield to maturity (YTM) of 9%. What is the maximum price that you would be willing to pay to buy this bond?

The timeline below represents an ordinary annuity of $50 per 40 periods using an effective semi-annual interest rate of 9%/2 = 4.5%.

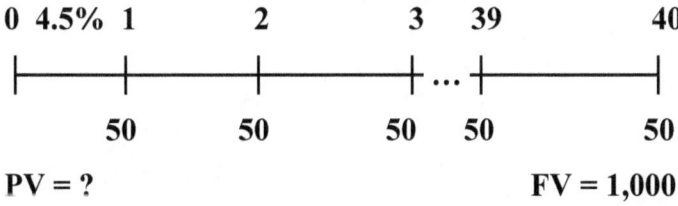

Copy the Example 8 worksheet and paste it to another tab.
The worksheet now looks like this:

	A	B	C
1	INPUTS	TVM	SOLUTION
2	5%	RATE	
3	4	NPER	
4	-2000	PMT	
5		PV	$7,091.90
6		FV	

Enter 4.5% in cell A2.

Enter 40 in cell A3.

Enter 50 in cell A4.

Enter 1000 in cell A6.

Now, the worksheet should look like this:

	A	B	C
1	INPUTS	TVM	SOLUTION
2	4.5%	RATE	
3	40	NPER	
4	50	PMT	
5		PV	-1,092.01
6	1000	FV	

Thus, the maximum price that you would be willing to pay for this bond is $1,092.01 in order for you to earn at least your required YTM of 9%.

Note that your required YTM was **less** than the stated bond coupon interest rate.

Whenever the required YTM is less than the coupon interest rate, the maximum price that you will be willing to pay will be more than the maturity value and vice versa.

Enter a name for this worksheet on the Tab, such as X13BONDVAL, and save it.

Example 14: NPER of Annuity PMTs for a Goal

In Example 5, a rather large lump sum payment of $30,000 for someone only 21 years old was insufficient to achieve a retirement goal of $1,000,000 when the interest rate was 4% compounded annually. In that example, we suggested that a feasible strategy would require periodic payments throughout a person's working career.

Suppose you are still 21 years old and feel that you will need at least $1,000,000 in savings to adequately fund your retirement. You plan to deposit $5,000 at the end of every year until you retire. If you can invest these periodic payments at 4% compounded annually, how long will it take to reach your financial goal of FV = $1,000,000?

The timeline below represents an ordinary annuity of $5,000 per year for N years at a 4% annual interest rate.

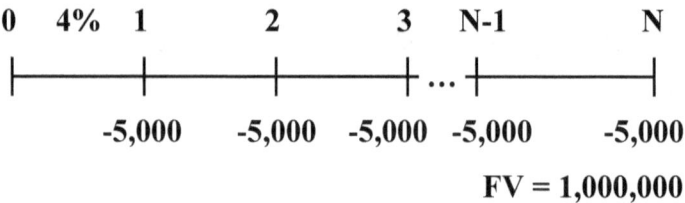

Copy the Example 5 worksheet and paste it into a new tab. The worksheet looks like this:

	A	B	C
1	INPUTS	TVM	SOLUTION
2	8%	RATE	
3		NPER	45.56
4	-30000	PMT	
5		PV	
6	1000000	FV	

Enter 4 in cell A2.

Enter -5000 in cell A4

The worksheet will then look like this:

	A	B	C
1	INPUTS	TVM	SOLUTION
2	4%	RATE	
3		NPER	56.02
4	-5000	PMT	
5		PV	
6	1000000	FV	

Thus, the number of periods required to achieve your financial goal is 56.02 years.

So, if you can save $5,000 at the end of each year starting at age 21, you can retire at age 77!

Enter a name for this worksheet on the Tab, such as X14NPERA, and save it.

Example 15: NPER of Annuity Due Goal PMTs

Redo Example 14 with annuity due payments. How much sooner can you retire?

The timeline below represents an annuity due of $5,000 per year for N years using an annual interest rate of 4%.

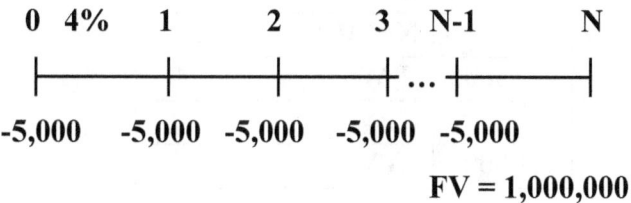

```
0  4%    1         2         3   N-1          N
├─────────┼─────────┼─────────┼ ... ┼─────────┤
-5,000   -5,000   -5,000   -5,000   -5,000
                            FV = 1,000,000
```

Copy the Example 14 worksheet and paste it into a new tab.

The worksheet looks like this:

	A	B	C
1	INPUTS	TVM	SOLUTION
2	4%	RATE	
3		NPER	56.02
4	-5000	PMT	
5		PV	
6	1000000	FV	

Modify the =*NPER(A2,A4,A5,A6)* formula in cell C3 to read =*NPER(A2,A4,A5,A6,1)* to change to annuity due mode.

The worksheet will now look like this:

	A	B	C
1	INPUTS	TVM	SOLUTION
2	4%	RATE	
3		NPER	55.14
4	-5000	PMT	
5		PV	
6	1000000	FV	

Thus, the number of periods now required to achieve your financial goal is 55.14 years.

So, if you can save $5,000 at the **beginning** of each year starting at age 21, you can retire at age 76 or approximately 1 year earlier than saving at the **end** of each year!

Enter a name for this worksheet on the Tab, such as X15NPERAD, and save it.

Example 16: Annuity PMTs for a Goal (Retire)

In the previous two examples, we determined that you would bc 77 (76) before you could retire when you made periodic savings deposits at the end (beginning) of the year.

Now suppose that you are willing to increase the size of the periodic payments at the end of each year so that you can retire at age 67, which is 46 years from today. If the interest rate is still 4% compounded annually and you still wish to achieve a FV = $1,000,000, how much must you deposit in your savings account at the end of each year for the next 46 years?

The timeline below represents an ordinary annuity of $? per year for 46 years using an annual interest rate of 4%.

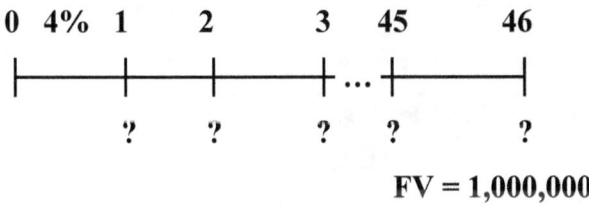

Copy the Example 14 worksheet into a new tab. The worksheet looks like this:

	A	B	C
1	INPUTS	TVM	SOLUTION
2	4%	RATE	
3		NPER	56.02
4	-5000	PMT	
5		PV	
6	1000000	FV	

Enter 46 in cell A3.

Delete the contents of cells A4 and C3.

Insert the function =*PMT(A2,A3,A4,A6)* into cell C4 and format the cell for currency. The worksheet will then look like this:

	A	B	C
1	INPUTS	TVM	SOLUTION
2	4%	RATE	
3	46	NPER	
4		PMT	-$7,882.05
5		PV	
6	1000000	FV	

Thus, the required annual PMT is $7,882.05.

Saving an additional $7,882.05 - $5,000 = $2,882.05 per year allows you to retire 77 – 67 = 10 years earlier.

Suppose you still wish to retire at age 67 but that you are age 30 now. This means that we must reset NPER to equal 37 instead of 46. So, in cell A2, enter 37 and the computer will immediately show the PMT to be -$12,239.57.

Deferring your savings plan for 9 years means that your annual deposits must increase by $12,239.57 - $7,521.89 = $4,717.68. Thus, it behooves you to start saving early for retirement!

Enter a name for this worksheet on the Tab, such as X16PMTA, and save it.

Example 17: Annuity Due Goal PMTs (Retire)

Redo Example 16 with annuity due payments.

The timeline below represents an annuity due of $? each year for 46 years using an annual interest rate of 4%.

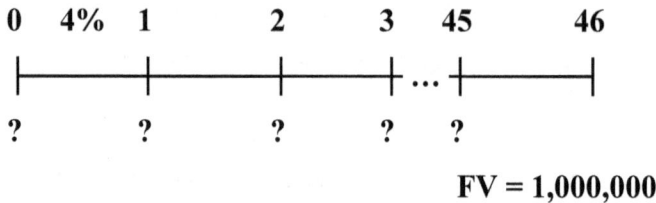

Copy the Example 16 worksheet and paste it to a new tab.

The worksheet looks like this:

	A	B	C
1	INPUTS	TVM	SOLUTION
2	4%	RATE	
3	46	NPER	
4		PMT	-$7,882.05
5		PV	
6	1000000	FV	

To change the calculation into annuity due mode, modify the formula in cell C4 to read *=PMT(A2,A3,A5,A6,1)*.

The worksheet should now look like this:

	A	B	C
1	INPUTS	**TVM**	SOLUTION
2	4%	**RATE**	
3	46	**NPER**	
4		**PMT**	-$7,578.89
5		**PV**	
6	1000000	**FV**	

Thus, with annuity due payments, the required PMT is $7,578.89.

Note that for any positive interest rate, the annuity due payment will be smaller than the ordinary annuity payment.

To be precise, each ordinary annuity payment must be the annuity due payment x (1 + periodic interest rate), *viz.*, $7,882.05 = $7,578.89 x 1.04.

Thus, once again we note that it behooves you to start saving early for retirement!

Enter a name for this worksheet on the Tab, such as X17PMTAD and save it.

CHAPTER 4

THE TVM CALCULATOR WORKSHEET

Introduction

Thus far in this book, the basics of using spreadsheets to solve time value of money (TVM) problems have been discussed. However, spreadsheets can do many things to expedite your calculations. Using IF statements, this chapter discusses how to create a single financial calculator TVM worksheet that can solve for any TVM variable.

This chapter concludes with a discussion of the use of IF statements in solving time value of money problems. IF statements enable Excel® to make decisions about what it should do with the data presented to it.

Copy the Example 1 FV worksheet and paste it into another Tab or an empty spreadsheet.

The worksheet looks like this:

	A	B	C
1	INPUTS	TVM	SOLUTION
2	5%	RATE	
3	4	NPER	
4		PMT	
5	7091.90	PV	
6		FV	$8,620.25

Modify the worksheet by inserting a new column B to the left of the existing column B by right clicking on the column B heading to get the drop-down menu and then clicking on insert. Choose Entire Column and click on OK.

Enter the label CODE in the new cell B1.
Enter the label TYPE in the new cell C7.

Enter the formula *=IF(B2=1,RATE(A3,A4,A5,A6,A7),"")* in cell D2. This is the Excel language format for IF statements, note the quote marks. If you use the RATE function menu, click on the cells where the data has been entered.

Enter the formula =*IF(B3=1,NPER(A2,A4,A5,A6,A7),"")* in cell D3. If you use the NPER function menu, click on the cells where the data has been entered.

Enter the formula =*IF(B4=1,PMT(A2,A3,A5,A6,A7),"")* in cell D4. If you use the PMT function menu, click on the cells where the data has been entered.

Enter the formula =*IF(B5=1,PV(A2,A3,A4,A6,A7),"")* in cell D5. If you use the PV function menu, click on the cells where the data has been entered.

Enter the formula =*IF(B6=1,FV(A2,A3,A4,A5,A7),"")* in cell D6. If you use the FV function menu, click on the cells where the data has been entered.

Enter 1 in cell B6.

The worksheet should now look like this:

	A	B	C	D
1	INPUTS	CODE	TVM	SOLUTION
2	5%		RATE	
3	4		NPER	
4			PMT	
5	7091.90		PV	
6		1	FV	$8,620.25
7			TYPE	

Note that the IF statements within the formulas of column D trigger the appropriate calculation functions whenever the code 1 appears in the appropriate row.

If cell B7 is left blank or has a zero entered within it, payments occur at the end of a period (ordinary annuity).

If a 1 is entered in cell B7, then payments occur at the beginning of a period (annuity due). This is the standard Excel function coding.

Enter a name for this worksheet on its tab, such as TVMCALCIF and save it.

CHAPTER 5

AMORTIZATION AND INTEREST CONVERSION

Introduction

A loan **amortization schedule** shows how much of each periodic loan payment is interest, and how much is principal repayment. It may take many years to completely pay off a loan, such as a 30-year mortgage, for example, and creating an amortization schedule by hand would be very tedious. However, Excel can do this quickly.

Because the periodic payment is comprised of both interest and principal, it is often referred to as a **blended payment**.

The amortization schedule typically also shows the beginning and remaining balance of the principal outstanding.

These topics are discussed in this chapter.

Example 18: Amortized Loan Components

Determine the interest and principal paid each year and the balance at the end of each year on a 4 year $10,000 amortizing loan that carries an interest rate of 10.5%. The payments are due at the end of each annual period.

The timeline below represents an ordinary annuity of $? each year for 4 years using an annual interest rate of 10.5%.

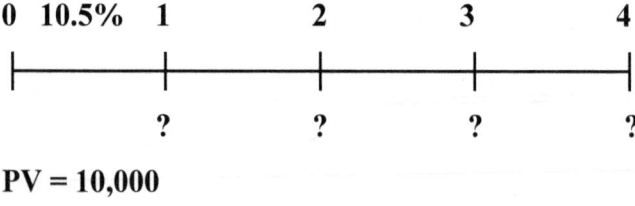

PV = 10,000

Copy the TVMCALCIF worksheet and paste it to a new tab. The worksheet looks like this:

	A	B	C	D
1	INPUTS	CODE	TVM	SOLUTION
2	5%		RATE	
3	4		NPER	
4			PMT	
5	7091.90		PV	
6		1	FV	$8,620.25
7			TYPE	

Enter 10.5 in cell A2.

Enter 4 in cell A3.

Enter 10000 in cell A5.

Enter 1 in cell B4.

Delete the contents of cell B6.

The worksheet should now look like this:

	A	B	C	D
1	INPUTS	**CODE**	**TVM**	SOLUTION
2	10.5%		**RATE**	
3	4		**NPER**	
4		**1**	**PMT**	-$3,188.92
5	10000		**PV**	
6			**FV**	
7			**TYPE**	

Thus, the periodic PMT is $3,188.92. This payment is a **blended payment** of interest and principal repayment.

We can now create an amortization schedule for this loan. To do so, add 5 more columns to the worksheet and label them as shown below:

	E	F	G	H	I
1	N	BEGIN	INTER	PRIN	END
2					
3					
4					
5					
6					

We use short columns to conserve space, but you could make the columns wider. You could also change the page layout from the default portrait mode to landscape mode by clicking on the Page Layout menu heading above the ribbon. Click on Orientation and then click on Landscape. This makes the page wider.

Enter 0, 1, 2, 3, and 4 in cells E2, E3, E4, E5, and E6.

Enter =A5 in cell I2.

Enter =I2 in cell F3.

Enter =F3*A2 in cell G3. (The $ signs tell Excel to permanently set the address for the RATE when you copy this formula into the other PRIN cells.)

Enter =-D4-G3 in cell H3. (The $ signs tell Excel to permanently set this address for PMT when you copy this formula into the other END cells. Since PMT is calculated as a negative number in cell D4, the minus sign before D4 is necessary to change PMT to a positive value.)

Enter =F3-H3 in cell I3.

Now copy cell F3 into the rest of the cells in the column. Then, do the same for columns G, H, and I.

If the cells are formatted for number with 2 decimal places and no separators, the worksheet should now look like this:

	E	F	G	H	I
1	N	BEGIN	INTER	PRIN	END
2	0				10000.00
3	1	10000.00	1050.00	2138.92	7861.08
4	2	7861.08	825.41	2363.51	5497.57
5	3	5497.57	577.25	2611.67	2885.90
6	4	2885.90	303.02	2885.90	0.00

Note that in this example, the final zero balance exactly pays off the loan. This is not always the case. The final blended payment and principal payment must be increased (decreased) if a rounding error has caused a small ending positive (negative) balance.

Enter a name for this worksheet on its Tab, such as X18AMORT, and save it.

Now we can import the worksheet into our word processor and make it a bit more attractive to the eye.

Amortization Schedule

N	Beginning Balance	Interest Portion	Principal Portion	Remaining Balance
0				10000.00
1	10000.00	1050.00	2138.92	7861.08
2	7861.08	825.41	2363.51	5497.57
3	5497.57	577.25	2611.67	2885.90
4	2885.90	303.02	2885.90	0.00

Example 19: U.S. Mortgage (Monthly Payments)

Suppose you are considering buying a new home in Florida. The bank quotes a nominal annual mortgage interest rate of 6% with monthly compounding and an amortization period of 30 years. Your dream home costs $300,000 and you have saved $60,000 for the down payment. Thus, you want to borrow $300,000 - $60,000 = $240,000. You want to make monthly payments because you are paid monthly. What is your monthly mortgage payment?

The timeline below represents a monthly ordinary annuity of $? for 30 years, this is 30 x 12 = 360 months. The nominal annual interest rate of 6% is based on monthly compounding.

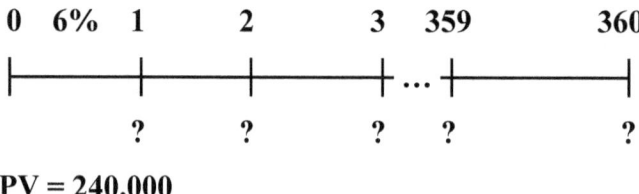

Copy the Example 18 worksheet and paste it into a new tab.

The worksheet looks like this:

	A	B	C	D
1	INPUTS	**CODE**	**TVM**	SOLUTION
2	10.5%		**RATE**	
3	4		**NPER**	
4		**1**	**PMT**	-$3,188.92
5	10000		**PV**	
6			**FV**	
7			**TYPE**	

Enter 6%/12 in cell A2. (The nominal annual rate of 6% is based on monthly compounding. Since we are also paying monthly, we can simply divide the nominal rate by 12 months to get the effective monthly rate.)

Enter 360 in cell A3.

Enter 240000 in cell A5.

The worksheet will then look like this:

	A	B	C	D
1	INPUTS	CODE	TVM	SOLUTION
2	0.5%		RATE	
3	360		NPER	
4		1	PMT	-$1,438.92
5	240000		PV	
6			FV	
7			TYPE	

Thus, the required monthly payment is $1,438.92.

Since this mortgage is for the lengthy period of 30 years, the first month blended payment is mostly interest and little principal repayment. With each monthly blended payment, a portion goes to repayment of principal. This means that the succeeding month will require a smaller interest payment and consequently a larger principal repayment. Thus, the last blended payment is virtually all principal repayment and little interest payment.

Enter a name for this worksheet on its Tab, such as X19USMORTPMT, and save it.

Example 20: Interest Conversion

Suppose that before you take out the mortgage in Example 19, you change jobs and are now paid semi-monthly (i.e. twice per month). You would now like to make your mortgage payments semi-monthly.

One might be inclined to calculate the effective semi-monthly rate as 6%/24 = 0.25%. However, since the nominal annual rate of 6% is based on monthly compounding, this would be incorrect. This rate of 0.25% compounded for two semi-monthly periods compounds to more than 0.5%, which is the effective monthly rate. That is: $1.0025^2 = 1.00500625 > 1.005$.

To find the correct semi-monthly rate, we need to construct an interest conversion worksheet.

Open a new tab with a name such as: **X20CONVERT**, and enter the following:

	A	B	C
1	INPUTS	**CONVERT**	SOLUTIONS
2		**NOM**	
3		**NPERY**	
4		**EFFECT**	
5		**NPMTY**	
6		**EPR**	

Enter the nominal annual rate of 6% in cell A2.

Enter 12 as the number of compounding periods per year (NPERY) in cell A3.

Insert the function *=EFFECT(A2,A3)* in cell C4 and format the cell for percentage with 8 decimal places.

The worksheet now should look like this:

	A	B	C
1	INPUTS	**CONVERT**	SOLUTIONS
2	6%	**NOM**	
3	12	**NPERY**	
4		**EFFECT**	6.16778119%
5		**NPMTY**	
6		**EPR**	

The **EFFECT** interest rate of 6.16778119% is the effective annual rate when the quoted or nominal rate is 6% with monthly compounding. That is, if we compound the effective monthly rate of 0.5% for 12 months, we would obtain the EFFECT. That is: $1.005^{12} = 1.0616778119$.

What we now need to find is an effective semi-monthly periodic rate (EPR), which compounds to 0.5% for 2 semi-monthly periods, *viz.*, $(1 + EPR)^2 = 1.005$.

When this EPR is compounded for 24 semi-monthly periods, it compounds to the EFFECT of 6.15778119%, *viz.*, $(1 + EPR)^{24} = 1.0616778119\%$.

Enter 24 in cell A5 as the number of payment periods per year (NPMTY).

Enter the formula =*(1+C4)^(1/A5)-1* in cell C6 and format the cell for percentage with 8 decimal places.

The worksheet should now look like this:

	A	B	C
1	INPUTS	**CONVERT**	SOLUTIONS
2	6%	**NOM**	
3	12	**NPERY**	
4		**EFFECT**	6.16778119%
5	24	**NPMTY**	
6		**EPR**	0.24968828%

The effective semi-monthly periodic rate (**EPR**) is given in cell C6 as 0.24968828%.

Make sure that you save the Example 20 worksheet, because it will be needed later.

Example 21: U.S. Mortgage (Semi-Monthly PMTs

Redo Example 19, except that you now want to make semi-monthly payments because you are paid semi-monthly. Recall that the bank quotes a nominal annual mortgage interest rate of 6% with monthly compounding and an amortization period of 30 years.

Your dream home costs $300,000 and you have saved $60,000 for the down payment. Thus, you want to borrow $300,000 - $60,000 = $240,000. What is your semi-monthly payment?

The timeline below represents an ordinary annuity of $? semi-monthly for 30 years; this is 30 x 24 = 720 periods. The nominal annual interest rate of 6% is based on monthly compounding, but we are making semi-monthly payments.

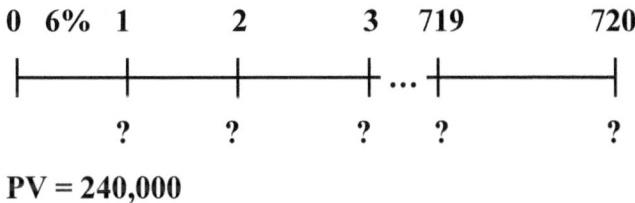

PV = 240,000

Copy the Example 19 worksheet and paste it into a new tab.

The worksheet looks like this:

	A	B	C	D
1	INPUTS	**CODE**	**TVM**	SOLUTION
2	0.5%		**RATE**	
3	360		**NPER**	
4		**1**	**PMT**	-$1,438.92
5	240000		**PV**	
6			**FV**	
7			**TYPE**	

Enter 0.24966828% in cell A2, which is the value of the
EPR in cell C6 of the **X20CONVERT** worksheet. Format
cell A2 as percentage with 8 decimal places.

Enter 720 in cell A3, which is the number of semi-annual
periods in 30 years.

Enter 240000 in cell A5.

The worksheet will then look like this:

	A	B	C	D
1	INPUTS	CODE	TVM	SOLUTION
2	0.24968828%		RATE	
3	720		NPER	
4		1	PMT	-$718.56
5	240000		PV	
6			FV	
7			TYPE	

Thus, the required periodic payment is $718.56.

Since you are making mortgage payments more frequently, you are repaying principal sooner. This means that the total interest charged over the life of the loan and in any month, will be **less** by making semi-monthly payments than making monthly payments.

This also means that total blended payments over the life of the loan and in any month, will be less by making the more frequent semi-monthly payments.

To see this, note that the semi-monthly blended payments for any month are 2 x $718.56 = $1,437.12 < $1,438.92, which is the blended monthly mortgage payment from Example 19.

Thus, the more frequently one pays, the lower the total interest and total blended payments will be.

Nevertheless, the more frequent blended payments are just a different annuity stream that is also time value equivalent to the amount borrowed.

Enter a name for this worksheet on its Tab, such as X21USMORTSMPMT, and save it.

One could also choose to make mortgage payments weekly or even bi-weekly. In the next example, we show how to calculate bi-weekly loan payments for a vehicle loan.

Example 22: Vehicle Loan with Bi-Weekly PMTs

Suppose you are considering buying a new SUV. The dealer quotes a nominal annual interest rate of 3% with monthly compounding and an amortization period of 6 years. Your SUV costs $30,000 and you want to borrow the full $30,000. You want to make bi-weekly payments because you are paid bi-weekly. What is your bi-weekly loan payment if you assume for simplicity that there are exactly 26 bi-weekly periods per year or 26 x 6 = 156 payments in 6 years?

The timeline below represents an ordinary annuity of $? for 156 periods using an annual interest rate of 3%.

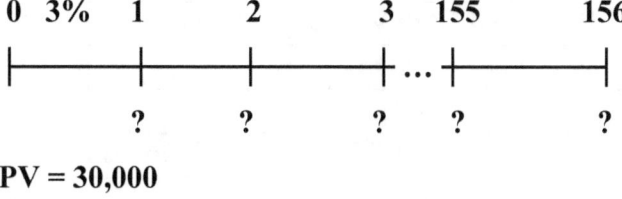

PV = 30,000

Copy the **X20CONVERT** worksheet and paste it into a new tab. The worksheet looks like this:

	A	B	C
1	INPUTS	**CONVERT**	SOLUTIONS
2	6%	**NOM**	
3	12	**NPERY**	
4		**EFFECT**	6.16778119%
5	24	**NPMTY**	
6		**EPR**	0.24968828%

Enter 3% in cell A2.

Enter 26 in cell A5.

The worksheet now looks like this:

	A	B	C
1	INPUTS	**CONVERT**	SOLUTIONS
2	3%	**NOM**	
3	12	**NPERY**	
4		**EFFECT**	3.04159569%
5	26	**NPMTY**	
6		**EPR**	0.11530705%

Copy and paste the Example 21 worksheet that looks like this:

	A	B	C	D
1	INPUTS	**CODE**	**TVM**	SOLUTION
2	0.24968828%		**RATE**	
3	720		**NPER**	
4		1	**PMT**	-$718.56
5	240000		**PV**	
6			**FV**	
7			**TYPE**	

Enter the EPR of 0.11530705% in cell A2.

Enter 156 in cell A3.

Enter 30000 in cell A5.

The worksheet should now look like this:

	A	B	C	D
1	INPUTS	**CODE**	**TVM**	SOLUTION
2	0.11530705%		**RATE**	
3	156		**NPER**	
4		1	**PMT**	-$210.23
5	30000		**PV**	
6			**FV**	
7			**TYPE**	

Thus, the periodic payment is $210.23. This payment is a blended payment of interest and principal repayment.

If you wish to construct a loan amortization schedule, follow the relevant steps in Example 18.

Enter a name for this worksheet on its Tab, such as X22BWPMT, and save it.

Example 23: Canadian Mortgage (Monthly PMTs

Suppose you want to buy a Canadian cottage on the shore of a quiet fishing lake in Northern Ontario. A Canadian bank quotes a nominal annual mortgage interest rate of 6% with semi-annual compounding for a 5-year term with amortization of 25 years. Your dream cottage costs $250,000 and you intend to pay $50,000 down. So, you want to borrow $200,000. Since you are paid a monthly salary, you want to make monthly mortgage payments. What is your monthly mortgage payment?

Unlike the U.S. customary monthly compounding of mortgage interest, Canadian banks must quote mortgage interest rates based on semi-annual compounding, **not** monthly compounding, to comply with the Bank Act of Canada. So, even when paying monthly, the payment frequency and the compounding frequency are different on all Canadian monthly mortgages.

Note that the 5-year term of the mortgage is shorter than the 25-year amortization period. This means that the bank is only fixing the interest rate for 5 years, but payments will be calculated as if the bank were fixing the rate for 25 years. In other words, the number of periods used in calculating the monthly payment will be 12 x 25 = 300. You will only make 12 x 5 = 60 payments before the monthly payments will be reset based on prevailing market rates and your outstanding balance or remaining principal.

Copy the Example 22 worksheet and paste it into a new tab. The worksheet looks like this:

	A	B	C
1	INPUTS	**CONVERT**	SOLUTIONS
2	3%	**NOM**	
3	12	**NPERY**	
4		**EFFECT**	3.04159569%
5	26	**NPMTY**	
6		**EPR**	0.11530705%

Enter 6% in cell A2.

Enter 2 in cell A3.

Enter 12 in cell A5.

The worksheet should now look like this:

	A	B	C
1	INPUTS	**CONVERT**	SOLUTIONS
2	6%	**NOM**	
3	2	**NPERY**	
4		**EFFECT**	6.09000000%
5	12	**NPMTY**	
6		**EPR**	0.49386220%

Copy and paste the Example 22 worksheet for the SUV loan. It looks like this:

	A	B	C	D
1	INPUTS	**CODE**	**TVM**	SOLUTION
2	0.11530705%		**RATE**	
3	156		**NPER**	
4		1	**PMT**	-$210.23
5	30000		**PV**	
6			**FV**	
7			**TYPE**	

Enter the EPR of 0.49386220% in cell A2.

Enter 300 in cell A3.

Enter 200000 in cell A5, which is the amount borrowed.

Now the worksheet should look like this:

	A	B	C	D
1	INPUTS	**CODE**	**TVM**	SOLUTION
2	0.49386220%		**RATE**	
3	300		**NPER**	
4		**1**	**PMT**	-$1,279.61
5	200000		**PV**	
6			**FV**	
7			**TYPE**	

Thus, the Canadian monthly mortgage payment will be $1,279.61.

Enter a name for this worksheet on its Tab, such as X23CDNMORTPMT, and save it.

CHAPTER 6

TVM CALCULATIONS:

UNEVEN CASH FLOWS

Introduction

This chapter discusses how to calculate the time value of money variables when cash flows are not equal.

Excel® can solve for the present value (PV), future value (FV), internal rate of return (IRR), and net present value (NPV) with built in functions capable of handling unequal cash flows.

This chapter discusses the calculation of present value, net present value and internal rate of return as well as the net advantage to leasing (NAL) and the NAL breakeven rate.

Example 24: PV of Uneven Cash Flows

Assume the following cash flows (CFs):

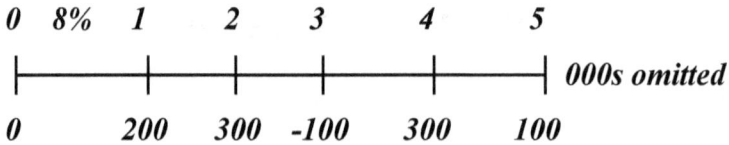

What is the present value (PV) of these cash flows (CFs) if the annual interest rate is 8%?

Copy the worksheet for Example 2 and paste it into a new tab.

The worksheet now looks like this:

	A	B	C
1	INPUTS	TVM	SOLUTION
2	5%	RATE	
3	4	NPER	
4		PMT	
5		PV	$7,091.90
6	-8620.25	FV	

Delete rows 3, 4, and 6 by right clicking on the row and choosing delete entire row on the drop-down menu.

The worksheet now looks like this:

	A	B	C
1	INPUTS	**TVM**	SOLUTION
2	5%	**RATE**	
3		**PV**	$7,091.90

Now add 7 more rows to our worksheet.

Enter the label Periods in cell A4.

Enter the label Cash Flows in cell B4.

Enter 0, 1, 2, 3, 4, and 5 in cells A5 through A10 and the worksheet will now look like this:

	A	B	C
1	INPUTS	**TVM**	SOLUTION
2	5%	**RATE**	
3		**PV**	$7,091.90
4	Periods	Cash Flows	
5	0		
6	1	200000	
7	2	300000	
8	3	-100000	
9	4	300000	
10	5	100000	

Enter 8% in cell B2.

Enter the formula =*NPV(A2,B6:B10)* in cell C3, and format it for currency. We could, of course, click on Formulas on top of the Ribbon, then click on Financial and then choose the NPV function from the list. The NPV function asks for the RATE and a set of Values. Thus, you should enter A2 and the array items B6, B7, B8, B9, and B10.

Now Excel will calculate the solution, which is $651,570.88, and the worksheet will look like this:

	A	B	C
1	INPUTS	**TVM**	SOLUTION
2	8%	**RATE**	
3		**PV**	$651,570.88
4	Periods	Cash Flows	
5	0		
6	1	200000	
7	2	300000	
8	3	-100000	
9	4	300000	
10	5	100000	

Enter a name for this worksheet on its Tab, such as X24PVUCF, and save it.

Example 25: PV of Embedded Annuities

Assume the following cash flows which contain embedded annuities:

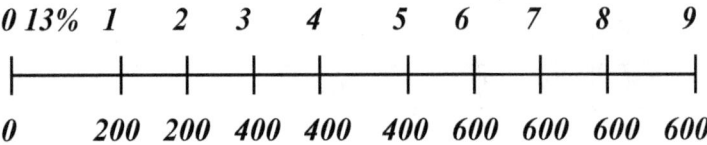

0 13% 1   2   3   4   5   6   7   8   9

0   200 200 400 400 400 600 600 600 600

What is the PV of these cash flows if the annual interest rate is 13%?

Copy the Example 24 worksheet and paste it into a new tab. The worksheet now looks like this:

	A	B	C
1	INPUTS	**TVM**	SOLUTION
2	8%	**RATE**	
3		**PV**	$651,570.88
4	Periods	Cash Flows	
5	0		
6	1	200000	
7	2	300000	
8	3	-100000	
9	4	300000	
10	5	100000	

We must now add 4 more rows by entering the numbers 6, 7, 8, and 9 in cells A11 to A14.

Enter 13% in cell A2.

Enter the numbers 200, 200, 400, 400, 400, 600, 600, 600, and 600 in cells B6 to B14.

Edit the number of cash flows in the cell C3 formula so that the four additional cash flows are taken into account, *viz.* *=NPV(A2,B6:B14)*.

The worksheet will now look like this:

	A	B	C
1	INPUTS	**TVM**	SOLUTION
2	13%	**RATE**	
3		**PV**	$2,041.93
4	Periods	Cash Flows	
5	0		
6	1	200	
7	2	200	
8	3	400	
9	4	400	
10	5	400	
11	6	600	
12	7	600	
13	8	600	
14	9	600	

Thus, the net present value is $2,041.93. We must use the NPV function to calculate the PV of cash flows, which are not equal in each period, because the PV function only works for equal flows.

Enter a name for this spreadsheet on its Tab, such as X25PVEACF, and save it.

Example 26: IRR of an Investment

If you invest $10,000 today, you expect to receive the uneven set of cash flows shown in the timeline below:

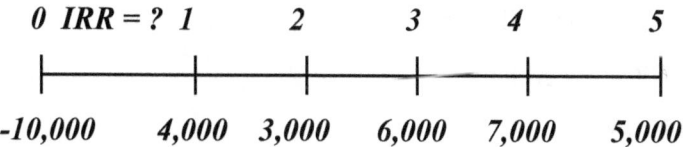

Should you make the investment if your required rate of return for investments of this degree of risk is 20%?

Copy the Example 24 worksheet and paste it into a new tab. The worksheet now looks like this:

	A	B	C
1	INPUTS	**TVM**	SOLUTION
2	8%	**RATE**	
3		PV	$651,570.88
4	Periods	Cash Flows	
5	0		
6	1	200000	
7	2	300000	
8	3	-100000	
9	4	300000	
10	5	100000	

Since this example already has 5 periods, all we have to do is change the data and enter the IRR formula in cell C2.

Delete the entries in cells A2 and C3.

Enter -10000 in cell B5.

Enter 4000 in cell B6.

Enter 3000 in cell B7.

Enter 6000 in cell B8.

Enter 7000 in cell B9.

Enter 5000 in cell B10.

Enter the formula =*IRR(B5:B10)* in cell C2.

Now the worksheet looks like this:

	A	B	C
1	INPUTS	**TVM**	SOLUTION
2		**RATE**	36.35%
3		**PV**	
4	Periods	Cash Flows	
5	0	-10000	
6	1	4000	
7	2	3000	
8	3	6000	
9	4	7000	
10	5	5000	

Since the computed IRR of 36.35% exceeds your required rate of return of 20%, the investment should be accepted because it will increase your wealth.

Enter a name for this worksheet on its Tab, such as X26IRR, and save it.

Most people who calculate the IRR of an investment also calculate the NPV of that investment.

Example 27: NPV of an Investment

Using the data from Example 26, you can also determine the NPV of this investment at your required rate of return of 20%.

Copy the Example 26 worksheet and paste it into a new tab.

The worksheet now looks like this:

	A	B	C
1	INPUTS	**TVM**	SOLUTION
2		**RATE**	36.35%
3		**PV**	
4	Periods	Cash Flows	
5	0	-10000	
6	1	4000	
7	2	3000	
8	3	6000	
9	4	7000	
10	5	5000	

All we need to do now is to enter 20% in cell A2 and insert the NPV formula *=NPV(A2,B6:B10)+B5* in cell C3.

You would naturally expect that Excel would use the same data to calculate NPV as it did to calculate IRR, but you would be wrong! Excel does not work that way! (We first discovered this error in 1980 while writing our first finance textbook).

To calculate the actual NPV, we must deduct the initial outlay of $10,000. Since this $10,000 is a *negative* cash inflow, it is stored in cell B6 as -10000. Adding the contents of cell B6 to the PV of the cash flows in cells B7 to B11, yields the actual NPV of $4274.05.

Now the worksheet looks like this:

	A	B	C
1	INPUTS	**TVM**	SOLUTION
2	20%	**RATE**	36.35%
3		**PV**	$4,274.05
4	Periods	Cash Flows	
5	0	-10000	
6	1	4000	
7	2	3000	
8	3	6000	
9	4	7000	
10	5	5000	

Thus, the net present value of this investment is $4,274.05. Since the PV of the cash flows exceeds the cost of the investment by $4,274.05 at a discount rate of 20%, you should make this investment because it will increase your wealth.

When an investment has normal cash flows (i.e. an outlay followed by a series of positive cash inflows) and is independent of any other investments, the decision to accept or reject the investment will be the same whether the IRR or NPV decision rule is used.

To be precise, NPV > 0 implies and is implied by IRR > required rate of return, leading to an increase in expected wealth by accepting the investment. NPV < 0 implies and is implied by IRR < required rate of return. In this case, one should reject the investment because accepting the investment would lead to a decrease in expected wealth.

In theory, one should be indifferent if NPV = 0, which implies and is implied by the IRR = required rate of return.

In practice, the authors recommend rejection of the investment in this case because there is a tendency to be overly optimistic when estimating future cash inflows.

Enter a name for this worksheet on its Tab, such as X27NPV, and save it.

Example 28: Net Advantage to Leasing (NAL)

Suppose you wish to buy or lease a Tesla electric sports car. The dealer offers to sell you the car for $100,000. You can borrow $100,000 to finance the car over 48 months at a 6% nominal annual interest rate with monthly compounding. This implies that the effective monthly interest rate is 6%/12 = 0.5%. Alternatively, the dealer will lease you the car. The 48 lease payments are $2,000 each, due at the beginning of each month with the last payment also due at the beginning of month 1 instead of month 48.

Having 2 advance payments is typical of most automobile leases. If you wish to buy the car at the end of the 48-month lease, a residual value payment of $20,000 is required.

Should you buy the car now or lease it and then exercise the option to buy at the end of the lease?

To decide whether to buy or lease, you should calculate the net advantage to leasing (NAL). The NAL is the purchase price of the car **less** the present value of the lease payments including the residual value. The discount rate will be the 0.5% effective monthly interest rate for the car loan.

The timeline for the cash flows of the NAL analysis is:

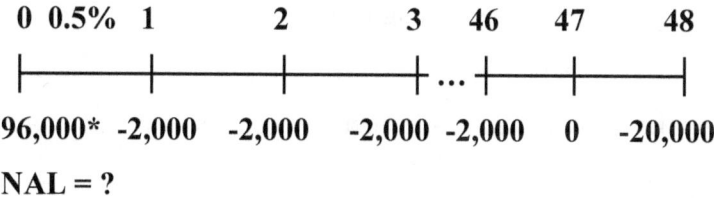

96,000* = $100,000 purchase price - $4,000 of lease payments due immediately

Note that the purchase price of the car always equals the PV of the blended monthly loan payments. For example, if the lender were charging a 9% nominal annual rate instead of 6%, the blended loan payments would be higher, but the PV of these higher loan payments based on the higher 9% rate would still be the purchase price of the car.

However, the PV of the fixed lease payments changes as the quoted loan rate changes. **The higher the loan rate, the lower is the PV of the lease payments.** Thus, leasing becomes more attractive as the loan rate rises.

Of course, as interest rates change in the economy as a whole, lease payments on new contracts can change. In this example, we focus on the fixed contract lease payments as we shop for loan rates among lenders.

Copy the Example 27 worksheet and paste it into a new tab.

The worksheet now looks like this:

	A	B	C
1	INPUTS	**TVM**	SOLUTION
2	20%	**RATE**	36.35%
3		**PV**	$4,274.05
4	Periods	Cash Flows	
5	0	-10000	
6	1	4000	
7	2	3000	
8	3	6000	
9	4	7000	
10	5	5000	

Modify this worksheet by adding rows 11 to 53 to hold the new data.

Enter the formula =*A10+1* in cell A11. Then copy cell A11 and paste it into the rest of the cells down to A53. This will create the period numbers from 6 to 48.

Enter 0.5% in cell A2.

Enter 96000 in cell B5.

Enter -2000 in cell B6.

Copy -2000 from cell B6 to cells B7 to B51.

Enter 0 in cell B52. (Do not leave it blank or you will not get the correct answer!)

Enter -20000 in cell B53.

Delete the entry in cell C2.

Modify the formula =**NPV(A2,B6:B10)+B5** in cell C3 to include the additional cells of data by changing B10 to B53 so the formula reads: =**NPV(A2,B6:B53)+B5**.

The worksheet now looks like this:

	A	B	C
1	INPUTS	**TVM**	SOLUTION
2	0.5%	**RATE**	
3		**PV**	-$1,746.34
4	Periods	Cash Flows	
5	0	96000	
6	1	-2000	
7-50	2-45	-2000	
51	46	-2000	
52	47	0	
53	48	-20000	

The NAL is simply the NPV of the above cash flows calculated at the effective monthly interest rate of 0.5%.

Thus, the NPV = -$1,746.34. Since the NAL is negative in this example, it is recommended that you buy the car for $100,000.

Enter a name for this worksheet on its Tab, such as X28NAL, and save it.

Example 29: NAL Breakeven Interest Rate

Using the data from Example 28, calculate the IRR that makes the NAL equal zero.

Copy the Example 28 worksheet and paste it into a new tab. The worksheet looks like this:

	A	B	C
1	INPUTS	**TVM**	SOLUTION
2	0.5%	**RATE**	
3		**PV**	-$1,746.34
4	Periods	Cash Flows	
5	0	96000	
6	1	-2000	
7-50	2-45	-2000	
51	46	-2000	
52	47	0	
53	48	-20000	

Enter the formula =*IRR(B5:B53)* cell C2.

Now the worksheet looks like this:

	A	B	C
1	INPUTS	**TVM**	SOLUTION
2	0.5%	**RATE**	0.56805925%
3		**PV**	-$1,746.34
4	Periods	Cash Flows	
5	0	96000	
6	1	-2000	
7-50	2-45	-2000	
51	46	-2000	
52	47	0	
53	48	-20000	

The RATE of 0.56805925% in cell C2 of the worksheet is the effective monthly IRR. Thus, the nominal annual breakeven interest rate based on monthly compounding is 12 x 0.56805925% = 6.81671105%.

The interpretation of this result is that for all nominal annual interest rates **above** 6.81671105%, **leasing will be more attractive because the NAL will be positive**. For all interest rates **below** 6.81671105%, **buying will be more attractive because the NAL will be negative**.

We have already shown that 6% < 6.81671105% gives a **negative** NAL in Example 28.

Let us obtain a positive NAL result by using 9% > 6.81671105%, which means that the effective monthly rate is 9%/12 = 0.75%. Replace 0.5% in cell A2 with the new value of 0.75%.

Now the worksheet looks like this:

	A	B	C
1	INPUTS	**TVM**	SOLUTION
2	0.75%	**RATE**	0.56805925%
3		**PV**	$4,463.09
4	Periods	Cash Flows	
5	0	96000	
6	1	-2000	
7-50	2-45	-2000	
51	46	-2000	
52	47	0	
53	48	-20000	

Thus, the revised NAL = $4,463.09. **Since the NAL is now positive, leasing is preferred.**

Enter a name for this worksheet on its Tab, such as X29NALBE, and save it.

SUGGESTED READINGS

If you are interested in learning more about solving time value of money problems, we suggest:

Brigham, E. & Ehrhardt, M. (2017) *Financial Management: Theory & Practice, 15th Edition,* Mason, OH: South-Western Cengage.

Brigham, E., Kahl, A. & Rentz, W. (1982) *Canadian Financial Management: Theory and Practice*, Toronto, ON: Holt, Rinehart & Winston of Canada.

If you are interested in learning more about Excel, we suggest:

Jelen, B. (2015) *Excel 2016 in Depth*. Indianapolis, IN: Que.

Walkenbach, J. (2015) *Excel 2016 Bible.* Hoboken, NJ: Wiley.

NOTES

www.ingramcontent.com/pod-product-compliance
Lightning Source LLC
Chambersburg PA
CBHW051535170526
45165CB00002B/739